Jesus, Our Hope

"Who can this be? Even the wind and the sea obey him."
Mark 4:41

The Benedictine Nuns of Turvey Abbey

Additional material by Mark Poulter

McCrimmons
Great Wakering Essex England

First published in 2000 by
McCRIMMON PUBLISHING CO LTD
10-12 High Street, Great Wakering, Essex SS3 0EQ
Telephone: 01702 218956
Fax: 01702 216082
Email: mccrimmons@dial.pipex.com
Web site: www.mccrimmons.co.uk

© 1999 The Benedictine Nuns of Turvey Abbey

Jesus, Our Hope   ISBN 0 85597 612 8

Jesus, Our Light   ISBN 0 85597 611 X
Jesus, Our Way   ISBN 0 85597 613 6

Edited and additional information by Mark Poulter
All images are taken from original paintings by the Benedictine
Nuns of Turvey Abbey, part of the *Jesus, Our Life series of posters*.
Typeset in Frutiger Light 11.5/13.5pt, 10/12pt and ITC Fenice
Regular Italic 24/26pt
Printed by Thanet Press., Margate, Kent

Contents

Introduction/Using this booklet 4–5
1. Zacchaeus 6–7
2. Jesus blesses the children 8–9
3. Jesus heals the sick 10–11
4. Martha and Mary 12–13
5. The Prodigal Son 14–15
6. The Lost Sheep 16–17
7. The Two Sons 18–19
8. The Sower 20–21
9. The widow's mite 22–23
10. The Samaritan woman by the well 24–25
11. The paralytic let down through the roof . . 26–27
12. Jesus calms the storm 28–29
Teaching guide 30
Table of themes 31

Jesus, Our Hope
The Ministry of Our Lord

Introduction
The stunning set of 12 posters which accompany this book follows the Ministry of Our Lord in a colourful and symbolic presentation of his miracles, parables and other events. God's love is made visible in Jesus' option for the poor, the sinners, the weak, the sick, the marginalised, the underdogs and the failures. In his Sermon on the Mount, Jesus summarised the blessedness of those whom the world would not normally regard as blessed, and he lived what he taught. By following his example we can build our own faith and look forward in hope.

Using this booklet
This booklet is designed to help teachers, catechists, R.E. co-ordinators and others to make the most of these beautiful images. On each page the artist has sought to describe her inspiration for each painting by reflecting on the relevant scripture references. We have also included:

- a picture of the poster;
- a quote from scripture; and,
- questions for discussion.

Page 31 of this booklet includes a cross-reference to themes and topics, such as those included in popular education programmes like *Here I Am* and *Walk With Me*. You may also wish to use some of the ideas that follow.

Discussion and teaching
The Questions for Discussion included in this booklet are designed to help teachers and catechists develop the responses of children to these well-known Bible stories. If you have time, we suggest you look up the scriptural reference yourself and reflect on it. Why not use a piece of the text as a heading for a display or a starting point for a session? And if you are stuck for time, you may want to use the scriptural quote we have selected. We do not aim to offer formulaic lessons and hope you will adapt and alter the material to suit the needs of the children in your care.

Display and decoration
The vibrant and striking colours of the paintings means they are ideally suited to display in Church, on notice-boards, as the centre piece of an R.E. display or prayer table/altar, or around school. You may wish to copy or type out one or more of the Questions for Discussion on each page and arrange them with the poster/s to make your displays more interactive and appealing to children and adults alike.

Assemblies and services
The posters are ideal for use in assemblies and services. You may want to display them as a basis for discussion or as a stimulus for prayer or reflection. They will also add colour and meaning to Bible stories read or acted out in the parish or school.

Prayer and meditation
A striking visual image often helps people to pray, meditate or reflect. You could use one or more of the posters as a focal point for an altar/prayer table or as the centre piece of a prayer service. This set of posters is particularly suited to themes such as Forgiveness and Reconciliation, Tolerance, the Nature of the Kingdom of God, and the Power of the Holy Spirit. (Please see page 31 for more themes.)

Creative writing and artwork
The rich and vivid colour of these illustrations, combined with the powerful imagery, makes them an ideal starting point for creative work. Why not use them to provoke thought and discussion before writing poetry or prayers? Or how about asking children to copy or re-design an image as part of their art work?

And finally...
Why not share your ideas and experiences with us?

We are always interested in finding out what works well and what materials you need to better fulfil your ministry.

Contact us at:
MCCRIMMONS, Freepost CL2425,
Southend-on-Sea, Essex, SS3 0BR
01702-218956 (phone)   01702-216082 (fax)
mccrimmons@dial.pipex.com (email)
www.mccrimmons.co.uk (Web site)

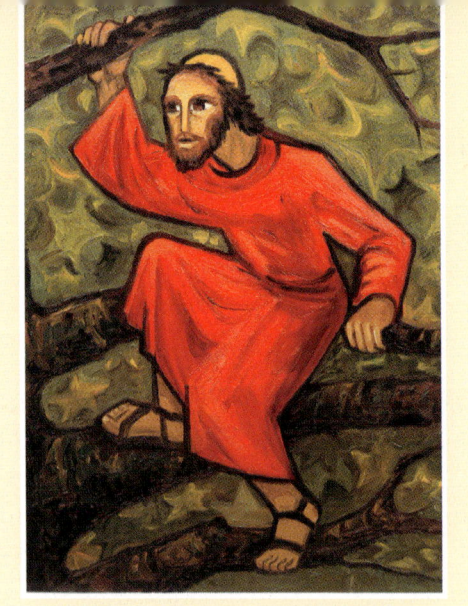

Imagine yourself sitting under the cool shade of a sycamore tree, just inside the gates of the city of Jericho. You've been sitting there since early morning. Jesus is on his way and you want to be sure to see him. More and more people are gathering. Listen to the people shouting and laughing and telling stories about the amazing things that Jesus has been doing.

Everybody is happy and laughing, except for one man who has a very sad face. Look at him now. His name is Zacchaeus. You wonder what he is doing as he doesn't often join in with other people. He is usually too busy counting his money.

Listen, people are starting to cheer. Jesus is here! Everybody is starting to push to get close to Jesus. You stay close by your tree. You can feel someone pushing beside you. Perhaps it is one of your friends. It's Zacchaeus! He's pushing everybody out of the way because he is so small that he can't see. Now he's climbing your sycamore tree.

Jesus has stopped right by Zacchaeus. They are looking right at one another.
The crowd has gone silent and you can hear your own heart beating very fast. What is Jesus going to say?

"Come down Zacchaeus," says Jesus. "I want to come to your house." Watch Zacchaeus as he jumps down. There's dust everywhere!

Jesus and Zacchaeus have disappeared. What do you think they are talking about? What would you like to say to Jesus if he came to your house?

1 Zacchaeus

Luke 19: 1–10

Zacchaeus was a rich man but, having acquired his wealth dishonestly, he was not popular. He was, however, all eagerness to see Jesus. He left his expensive cloak at the bottom of the tree and climbed up, like any street-urchin, making a fool of himself. Probably, Jesus had already seen this little man before he reached his perch on the tree, and touched his heart. We see him here at the moment when Jesus looked up to him and invited himself to his house. Zacchaeus can hardly believe his ears and eyes! Down he jumps and makes a wholehearted submission. His conversion is complete: the sinner is rescued and set on the path to wholeness and blessedness.

'He has gone to stay at a sinner's house.'

Luke 19: 7

Questions for discussion

How do you feel when you do something wrong?

What is it like to be unpopular?

Why do you think Zacchaeus wanted to see Jesus?

Why did Jesus decide to stay at Zacchaeus' house?

What should we do if other people hurt us?

Is it always easy to forgive people when they have hurt you?

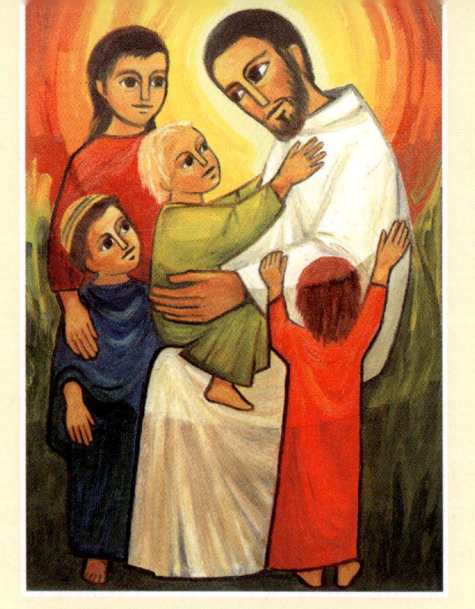

Imagine you are one of the children in the picture. Jesus has been talking to the grown-ups in your village all day. It's early evening and the sun is just starting to set. Nearly the whole village has ended up in the market place. They've been sitting, listening to Jesus. You've never known everybody to be so quiet.

Jesus talked about his father and the Kingdom of Heaven. He said the Kingdom of Heaven isn't a place – it's a way you have to be. Jesus says it is time to stop being big and powerful. Start being happy, kind and doing what you know is right.

The crowd is starting to move closer to Jesus. Some mothers are carrying their babies and asking him to touch and bless them. Jesus looks tired but friendly.

Make your way to Jesus now. Squeeze past people. You may even need to get down on your hands and knees and crawl through people's legs! You are getting closer. Listen to the children laughing and giggling.

At last you reach Jesus. He puts his hand gently on your shoulder and for a moment you can't hear the shouting and laughing – it's just you and Jesus. The noises around you are changing. You can hear angry shouting. The disciples are cross. They think Jesus should be left alone.

Look at Jesus' face. What does he think? You remember what Jesus said about the Kingdom of Heaven and not believing you are more important than someone else. Have the disciples understood this?

You decide it is time to go but know you will see Jesus again. What will you say next time you meet?

2 Jesus blesses the children

Mark 10: 13–16   Luke 18: 15–17

Zacchaeus was like a child, dropping his dignity in order to catch a glimpse of Jesus. The condition of entering the Kingdom of Heaven is to become like a child (*Luke 18: 16-17*) and Zacchaeus entered it there and then. Jesus' followers were familiar with his insistence on the need to become like children again in simplicity and trust, newly born (*John 3: 3*); only then can we truly call God our Father and be brothers and sisters of Jesus, sharing his life. Jesus identified with the children he gathered around him, in order that they might identify with him. Here the Kingdom of God has come about. It is as simple and close to us as that. Yet to be small and insignificant has never been an attractive option, and is still less so today.

'Let the little children come to me'

Mark 10: 14

Questions for discussion

How do you feel when someone is rude to you?

What does it feel like when adults stop you from doing something you want to do?

Are adults always right?

Does anyone make you feel small? Why?

What can you do to show people you are special?

How would Jesus like you to behave?

Why is Jesus your special friend?

Imagine you are travelling along a dusty road with your whole family.
It's sunset and the sky is filled with orange and yellow. You've been travelling all day. At last you've made it.

Your family has heard about Jesus. They have heard he is able to cure the sick just by touching them. Look at the adults. They look tired and weary. They have been carrying your sister for hours. She is very sick. Your sister lifts her head. Watch as she smiles. She doesn't know just how sick she is.

There are crowds of people here, just to see Jesus. Everyone is silent. A blind man is sitting by a tree. He calls out, asking for Jesus. Watch carefully as Jesus walks up and, without a sound, puts his hands on the man's eyes. Still there is no sound. No-one speaks. The blind man and Jesus hug each other and the man walks away without his stick.

You've been so busy watching the blind man that you haven't noticed Jesus kneeling by your sister. He is holding her hand. Your sister is gazing at Jesus and starting to say something. What is she saying?

Watch as Jesus helps her to stand up. She holds his hand very tightly and won't let go. Your whole family is watching in amazement. Look at their faces.

All of a sudden, your sister runs up and throws her arms around you. Jesus sits down and watches. Go up to Jesus and thank him for what he has done.
Is there anything that you would like him to do for you?

3 Jesus heals the sick

Mark 10: 13–16   Luke 4: 40–4

Jesus' divinity shines out most clearly in his healing of the sick, his raising of the dead, and his approach to the outcast and unclean. Jesus is the Resurrection and Life (*John 11: 25*) and God is at work here with the same power by which Jesus was raised from the dead. "I felt a power going out of me", said Jesus when a sick woman touched his cloak in faith (*Luke 8: 46*). It is faith that established the link with Jesus' healing power. Jesus took upon himself the burdens of all sufferers and carried them to Calvary (see *Isaiah 53: 4-5*). He took their sickness upon himself and gave them his very own health. We find this beautifully illustrated in the story of the cleansing of the leper in Mark 1: 40-45. After healing the leper Jesus could no longer go about freely among the people: he had to go away to a lonely place. He became an outcast in the leper's place.

'Laying his hands on each he cured them.'

Luke 4: 40

Questions for discussion

How do you feel when you are ill?

Have you ever cared for someone else who is sick? Is it an easy job?

How do you feel when you have no friends?

What can you do to be a friend to other people?

How do we know that Jesus was so powerful?

Why do you think Jesus spent so much of his time looking after the poor and healing the sick?

Look at the picture in front of you. Look carefully at all the different colours that have been used.
Now choose one face and study the eyes. Why do you think the artist has painted them like that?
Now look carefully at the other two faces.

Imagine it is evening time and you are sitting a little distance from a house where the door has been left open. You can just about peer inside and see what is happening. It is Martha and Mary's house. They are good friends of Jesus and like to spend time with him.

Martha has been busy all day preparing the food. Mary has been busy too. She's been thinking about all the things she wants to say to Jesus.
Jesus has arrived at last. He sits straight down and so does Mary. They begin to talk.
Look closely at their faces. What do you think they are saying?

The food is nearly ready and Martha is getting cross. Why doesn't Mary help?
She is so busy talking to Jesus but what is she saying? Jesus is smiling. He looks at Martha, and then across at Mary.

Watch as he tells Martha not to worry. Martha finds this hard. She still looks a little cross but Mary doesn't seem to notice at all. She just keeps looking at Jesus.

If Jesus came to your house, what would you tell him about?

4 Martha and Mary

Luke 10:38-42

Every household or community has its expert cook, the person who puts all loving care into the preparation of meals, beautifully served. That was Martha. Mary was rather more the type to curl up with a book, quite ready to help when needed but getting totally absorbed when anything held her interest. In John 12: 1-8 we read about another meal at the sisters' house and see the difference of characters confirmed. Here too, Jesus defends Mary. Not that he did not appreciate Martha's service; he rather supported the weaker one who tended to be misunderstood and blamed, if not by Martha, then by Judas. Martha will get plenty of compliments from the guests anyway. However, Martha too would have liked to hear what Jesus had to say. She is somewhat annoyed as she suggests to Jesus that Mary might give her a hand. Jesus' answer seems a bit unfair to her. Luke does not tell us what happened afterwards, but it is a good guess that Mary did roll up her sleeves after the guests had gone, and that both sisters had their share of peace and joy Jesus came to bring.

'You worry and fret about so many things, and yet few are needed, indeed only one.'

Luke 10: 41

Questions for discussion

Is there any one person in your home who does most of the housework? Who is it?

What could you do to help out at home?

Why did Jesus tell Martha to stop worrying?

Was Jesus pleased that Mary listened to him? Why?

How can you show Jesus you are listening to him?

Imagine you are a servant in a large house. You've been asked to prepare an enormous feast. Your master's son was lost and now he is found. You've been working for your master for some time and have got to know his two sons. One is called David, the other Esau.

A few months ago David left for a far away country. Everyone was sad, including you. David left with a large purse of money. Your master seemed upset and stopped talking.

But today everything has changed. Your master spotted David a long way off, making his way slowly home. David's clothes were dirty and torn. His feet were cut and bruised and he had no shoes. Your master couldn't believe his eyes.
He ran out to meet him. There they are in front of you now. David keeps his head bowed and doesn't dare look at his father's face.

Your master holds David tightly. Nobody speaks. Watch as David goes down on his knees to say sorry. His father touches his shoulder and pulls him to his feet. David is completely forgiven. He has wasted his father's money and turned his back on his family but none of that matters any more.

Watch as David's face begins to change. He knows he is really forgiven. They walk off to begin the celebrations.

Esau has been out in the fields and has heard all the commotion. He's very angry. Why is all this fuss being made of his brother? How can you help Esau understand what has happened? Talk to him now and see what happens.

Did you persuade him to come to the party? Watch everybody in the room enjoying themselves. Is there anything you want to celebrate?

5 The Prodigal Son

Luke 15: 11-32

The stories Jesus told us and his dealings with people, repeatedly show that Christianity is the world upside down. Here a young good-for-nothing gets feasted in preference to his well-behaved, hardworking elder brother. God's ways are not our ways, and his thoughts are not our thoughts (see *Isaiah 55:8*). Most probably it was the Prodigal's memory of a loving, understanding father that helped him to carry out his brave decision to return home and admit his fault. And his hopes were fulfilled beyond his wildest dreams. Twice the father gives his reason for this huge celebration: this son was dead and has come back to life. Jesus identifies with the sinner-son. He too was dead and came back to life, and we all may follow him there.

'Your brother here was dead and has come to life; he was lost and is found.'

Luke 15: 32

Questions for discussion

Have you ever felt jealous of someone else? When?

How does it feel when someone else is getting all the praise or attention?

Can you think of a time when somebody hurt you or said something nasty to you?

Is it difficult to forgive people who upset and hurt us?

How do we know that God will always forgive us?

Are you ready to forgive the people who have hurt you?

Imagine your are sitting by yourself on a hillside. It's a warm day and the sun is bright, too bright too look at. In the distance you can see a familiar figure – it's your brother Joshua. He's a shepherd here in Judea.

One day you hope to become a shepherd just like your brother. He is so brave and protects his precious sheep. Joshua even sleeps out on the hillside just to make sure no-one comes at night to steal the sheep.

Watch Joshua walk slowly through the sheep. They all know him so there is no need for them to feel scared and run away. Joshua looks at each sheep in turn. They are all different and yet he knows them all. Look at their faces. Can you tell them apart?

Watch Joshua as he starts to count his sheep. It must be a hard job – they keep moving! Look more closely at Joshua's face. He is starting to look worried. Something's wrong. What is it?

One of the sheep is missing! Joshua must find it. It's starting to get dark and the sheep could be in danger.

Joshua sets off in search, leaving the others to find the one precious sheep that is missing. Rest yourself against a big tree, close your eyes and imagine Joshua's journey.

Open your eyes and see Joshua standing right in front of you. He's smiling the most enormous grin. Look! He's carrying the lost sheep on his shoulders. The sheep is safe at last and now Joshua doesn't have to worry any more. He really is a good shepherd.

6 The Lost Sheep

Luke 15: 3-7   Matthew 18: 10-14

Sheep are gregarious creatures; they like to stay together with their fellows and dread being left alone. If someone is missing, it is a matter of life and death to find the stray one. In Luke's account the lost sheep stands for the sinner about whose conversion the angels rejoice. In Matthew it signifies a child, the least of God's people but great in God's eyes, worth searching and bringing back to the flock because "their angels always see my Father's face." In both cases angels come into the picture, and sinners are made to share the innocence of sheep, child and angel. Small wonder that the shepherd rejoices.

'It is never the will of your Father in heaven that one of these little ones should be lost.'

Matthew 18: 14

Questions for discussion

Why was the shepherd worried about his missing sheep?

Have you ever been lost?

What does it feel like to be alone?

How do you feel when you find something that has been missing for a long time?

How do you know that God is always looking after you?

Imagine you are the father of two sons. You are the owner of a large vineyard. It's harvest time – the busiest time of the year. Every branch in your vineyard is full of large, dark grapes. You haven't been able to find enough workers to pick them all so you will have to ask your sons.

Your sons are very different. Reuben is full of life and always asking questions. Joshua is quiet and a little serious. He takes life slowly.

It's early morning and still cool. You take a walk around the vineyard looking for your sons. What do you see on the way?

You find Joshua. He's sitting in the courtyard and looks like he has been day-dreaming. Put your hand on his shoulder and watch as he opens his eyes. "Son, will you come and work in my vineyard?" you ask.

"No father, not today, I'm too tired," Joshua replies. You walk away disappointed.

In the distance you can hear laughing and talking. Reuben is sure to be among the crowd. He's always full of energy and ideas. "Father," shouts Reuben. "Come and meet my friends."

Tell Reuben you need help in the vineyard today. Reuben smiles and says he will be delighted to help. You walk away pleased. When you have walked some distance turn and see that Reuben is still with his friends. He hasn't gone to the vineyard after all.

Next you meet Joshua. His hands and clothes are covered in grape juice. He has been to the vineyard after all! When God asks us to do something it can be hard to say yes. Listen carefully. What do you think God is asking you to do?

7 *The Two Sons*

Matthew 21: 28-32

This poster could be read like a comic strip. Both sons have heard their father's request. The one on the left says 'yes', picks up his baskets, but does not go to the vineyard. The boy on the right says 'no' and walks away, changes his mind and does go to the vineyard. Both examples give life stories in a nutshell. God does not take 'no' for an answer and will surely stir the first boy up out of his lethargy and send him to the vineyard, giving him his full wages, even if he arrives at the eleventh hour (Matthew 20: 1-16).

'So those who are last will be first, and those who are first will be last.'

Matthew 20: 16

Questions for discussion

Have you ever broken a promise? What happened?

How does it feel to be let down by a friend?

Have you ever made a decision about something and then changed your mind? What happened?

How does God want you to behave?
How can you find out?

What will you do to show God you love him?

Imagine yourself sitting by the edge of the field in the picture. Feel the warm sun beating down on your head, shoulders and back. Now touch the rich brown soil. It's warm from the sun. Dig a little until you feel the cool, damp earth underneath the surface.

Now watch the sower moving slowly backwards and forwards scattering the tiny seed. Some seed falls by your feet. Pick it up and spend some time looking at it. Now blow it and see where it lands.

The sower is like God. God scatters his love all around us. Sometimes we can see this and we can help God's love to grow inside ourselves.

Think of a time when you have helped God's love to grow.

Sometimes it's difficult for God's love to grow. Sometimes we just don't give it a chance. Sometimes we don't listen to what God wants.

Study the picture again and take a close look at the scattered seed. Try to imagine what the field will look like when everything has grown. Try to imagine the wonderful colours and smells of a field full of crops.

Now try to imagine what the world will be like if your friends and everybody in your family, helps God's love to grow.

8 The Sower

Matthew 13: 4-9, 18-23

This painting shows the sower sowing his seed, with the harvest already ripe in the background. Though the soil looks dark and lifeless and he is "sowing in tears", he knows that he will sing when he reaps (*Psalm 125: 5*). Here too we have the mystery of death and resurrection:

"A grain of wheat remains a solitary grain unless it falls into the ground and dies, but if it dies it bears a rich harvest." (*John 12: 24*)

Rich and abundant, we can witness the full flowering of the Kingdom of Heaven. Evil forces will thwart its growth but will not overcome it. In John 4: 36, Jesus invites us to the vision of the harvest already there, "so that the sower and reaper may rejoice together".

'Others fell on rich soil and produced their crop.'

Matthew 13: 8

Questions for discussion

What happens to the seed that falls on the path/rock/thorns? Why?

What does a plant need to grow well?

Why did the good soil produce the best crop?

What do you need to grow well?

How can you be like the rich soil in the parable?

How can you help to spread the Good News of Jesus?

Take some time to look carefully at the picture. What do you think the people are doing?

Imagine yourself sitting in a dark corner in the temple. Rest against one of it's huge pillars. The stone is cool. Watch carefully as people come and go, bringing their offerings to the temple.

You can see someone holding a large, shiny coin. He's looking at it carefully before he puts it into the collecting box. What is he thinking?

Feel in your pockets to see if you have any coins to offer.

You watch as out of the darkness an old lady appears. You've seen her before. She is very poor but every week she brings something to the temple. Today she looks really tired and old. Watch closely as she moves across the temple. Now look at her face. What do you see?

She puts her hand slowly and carefully into her deep pockets. When she pulls her hand out again it's tightly closed. She doesn't want to drop anything. She holds her hand over the collecting box and drops a single coin in. Listen to the sound it makes.

The old lady has given everything she had. Now imagine that you will walk over to the box and give everything you have.

Even if you have very little money, or no money at all, you can still give God all you have. Stop and spend a few moments thinking about ways you can give yourself to God.

9 The widow's mite
Mark 12: 41-44

Here too Jesus has no eye for the rich people offering money from their wealth. Like a spotlight his eyes focus on an unassuming figure, who simply comes to offer 'all she has to give', and this is of immense value in God's eyes. God himself has given us 'all he has to give' in Jesus (see *Romans 8:32*) and this is the pattern set for us to follow. The smallness of our self-giving, as long as it is 'all we have to give' is raised to the greatness of God's unfathomable gift to us: Jesus himself. It is the mystery of bread and wine: our gift to God becoming his gift to us, the pledge of eternal life.

'This poor widow has put more in than all who have contributed to the treasury;'

Mark 12: 43

Questions for discussion

What is it like to be poor?

What does a rich person look like?

Is it better to be rich or poor?

Why did Jesus say the widow had put in more than everyone else?

What gifts has Jesus given you?

What can you give to God?

Imagine you are alive at the time of Jesus and living in the town of Samaria. Every day around sunset you are sent to Jacob's well to fetch water. You like going because it gives you a chance to think. It also gives you time for some peace and quiet away from your noisy brothers and sisters.

You are almost at the well when you notice two people are sitting by the well talking. One of them looks like Jesus. Walk a little closer. Yes, you are quite certain – it's his kind face and the gentle way he is speaking which help you to recognise him.

Jesus is talking to a woman and asking for a drink of water. You hear the woman say that Jesus has no bucket. How can he get water! Perhaps Jesus would like to borrow your bucket!

You listen a little more and hear Jesus talking about living water. You are not sure what this means. Jesus isn't talking about the water you drink. He says that if you live like he loves and follow his teachings you will live forever. Think about all the times you have heard Jesus speak. What is his message for you?

Watch the woman's face as she talks with Jesus. How is she feeling? What would you say if Jesus told you to follow him?

The woman didn't realise she was talking to Jesus. She looks amazed because Jesus has been telling her things about herself. Jesus really knows her. Watch as she puts down her jar and hurries away to tell her friends she has met Jesus.

Jesus is still sitting by the well. Go and sit beside him. Is there anything you would like to ask him?

10 The Samaritan woman by the well

John 4: 4-30

Water is a precious commodity in the parched lands of the Bible. Water appears as both death-dealing and life-giving: Genesis 7: 2-23; Exodus 14: 26-28; Ezekiel 47: 8-12; Revelation 22: 1-2, to mention a few examples. It is the two-fold effect of Baptism: death to sin and life for God. Jesus is the Source of Living Waters and reveals himself as such to the Samaritan woman by the well. How much did she understand? Enough surely to kindle in her the thirst for that living water and ask for it, and in asking she received (*Matthew 7: 7*). That chance meeting with the Source of Living Water changed her life dramatically, and not only hers. John tells us that "many became believers because of what the woman had told them" (*John 4: 41*). There and then, she became his witness.

'Anyone who drinks the water that I shall give will never be thirsty again.'

John 4: 14

Questions for discussion

What do you use water for?

How does water make you feel?

Why do we need to drink lots of water?

Why was water used when you were baptised?

What promises were made when you were baptised?

What can you do for God to show that your baptism is important?

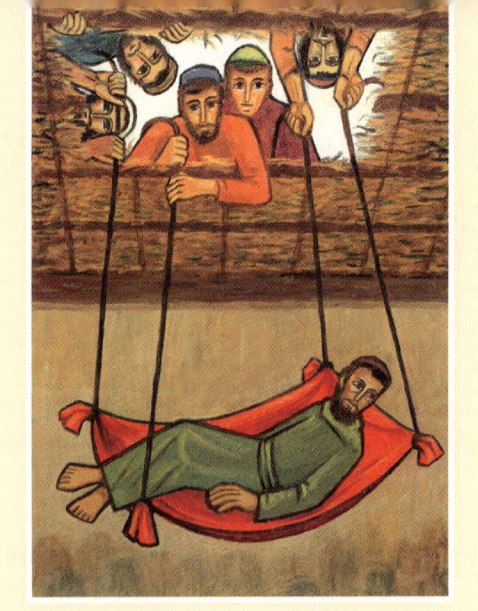

It's early afternoon and you have been out with the disciples all day. Jesus is away and you are wondering when he is coming back. Ahead of you is a large crowd of people shouting and laughing. They are making their way to a big house on the edge of town.

Someone shouts, "It's Jesus. He's back!" Everyone starts to run. There are clouds of dust everywhere. The crowd is pushing as everyone wants to get nearer. You notice Jesus' face is calm and gentle. He doesn't seem to mind that people are getting closer and closer.

Jesus closes his eyes and the crowd goes silent. He opens his eyes and begins to speak about his father. Right at the back you notice four men with a friend who is very sick. He is lying very still on a stretcher. They look anxious.

You watch carefully as they carry the stretcher around to the back of the house. No-one seems to have noticed. Somehow they manage to get on the roof, take off some of the parts and begin to lower their friend into the room.

Suddenly the crowd goes quiet. Jesus smiles. He touches the sick man's hand and says, "Your sins are forgiven."

Some people in the crowd start to look very cross but Jesus is still kneeling by the man. He says, "Stand up, my friend. Pick up your stretcher and go home."

The people are amazed. How can Jesus have such power. They start to praise God at the top of their voices. You stop and think. Is there anything you would like to praise God for?

11 The paralytic let down through the roof

Luke 5: 18-26

The opening up of the roof must have been a simple operation, not involving any damage to the owner's property. We can imagine the excitement of the friends on the roof, watching and waiting to see what Jesus' reaction would be to their unexpected jumping of the queue. Surely Jesus enjoyed their resourcefulness which was prompted by faith. He looked up and saw faith shining in those eager faces, and they got what they wanted. Though the pharisees and doctors of the law pricked their ears in dismay when Jesus forgave the man's sins, the paralytic's trust in Jesus was greatly enhanced, and he became ready to receive the gift of healing. What else could he do when he walked off, but praise God. Surely he was joined by a chorus from the roof!

'When Jesus saw how much faith they had, he said to the man "Your sins are forgiven my friend".'

Luke 5: 20

Questions for discussion

Have you ever seen anything strange happen? What happened?

What does it feel like when something amazing happens?

How do we know God is so powerful?

How can we show other people we are happy to believe in God?

Can you think of some good ways to praise God?

It's early evening and just starting to get dark. You've spent all day with the disciples, sitting by the lake listening to Jesus.

Jesus wants to cross to the other side. As the boat drifts on to the lake, the noise of the crowd dies away and you start to feel peaceful and safe.

But all of a sudden it becomes very dark and heavy black clouds fill the sky. The wind begins to blow and huge waves crash against the side of the boat. You don't feel safe anymore.

Where's Jesus? Isn't he afraid? Look at him resting his head on a cushion. Doesn't he care? Go over and try to wake him.

Jesus opens his eyes and smiles. The disciples are terrified as the waves continue to smash against the boat. One of them calls out, "Look, we're sinking!"

Jesus stands up. He looks at you for a moment and then out to sea and says, *"Quiet now! Be calm!"*

The roaring of the waves stops and the sea is silent. Your heart is beating so fast but the disciples begin to relax. The boat is gently rocking from side to side. Jesus looks at you and asks, *"Why were you so frightened?"*

You try to tell Jesus everything that makes you afraid. Jesus looks back and smiles. You know he has understood everything you have told him.

12 Jesus calms the storm

Mark 4: 36-41

"Greater than the roar of mighty waters, more glorious than the surgings of the sea, the Lord is glorious!" (*Psalm 92: 4*)
– an echo of so many proclamations of God's Lordship over the elements of his creation. The boat rocked by the waves recalls a well-known image of the Church. Jesus is present but asleep and not in the least worried about the fate of the boat and its occupants. And we for centuries remain the people of little faith, forgetting Jesus' promise to be with us until the end of time (*Mark 28: 2*), secure in the leadership of the Holy Spirit who will guide us in all the truth (*John 16: 13*), and yet another promise: "You will do greater things than these!" (*John 14: 12*). Jesus places so much trust in the people in the rocking boat. Can we dare to put our trust in him?

> 'Who can this be? Even the wind and the sea obey him.'
>
> Mark 4: 41

Questions for discussion

What does a storm look like?

How do you feel when there is a storm?

Have you ever been afraid of something? Why?

Can you think of some ways that God protects you?

How do we know that God is always with us?

How can you show that you trust God?

Teaching guide

At McCrimmons we recognise that planning with today's popular R.E. programmes is often a difficult and time-consuming task. This brief guide has been written to help you make the most of these posters without having to spend a long time looking for resources and information.

Here I Am & Walk With Me

The table on the opposite page is cross-referenced to the themes in the *Here I Am* and *Walk With Me* catechetical programmes. If you are short of time, we hope the table might provide a quick solution for teachers and catechists who are under pressure of work. The bold headings at the top refer to the stages of the R.E. programmes.

General themes

We have also included some general themes (under the *Others* heading) that may help you integrate the posters into other R.E. programmes. You may also want to adapt the posters and booklet material to suit the individual needs of your own school or parish.

Developing the material

If you have the opportunity, we recommend that you spend more time developing your own thematic index that suits the needs of your own unique situation. All the best R.E. teaching comes when the teacher or catechist has really thought about the needs of the children concerned and planned well with those needs in mind. We hope this table will be a useful starting point.

Title	N/R	ONE	TWO	THREE	FOUR	OTHERS
1. Zacchaeus	Communion, Change	Communion, Choices	Invitations	Change, Meals Bridges	Building Forgiveness	Tolerance,
2. Jesus blesses children						K. of H.
3. Jesus heals the sick						Healing
4. Martha and Mary				Meals	Relationships	Friendship,
5. The Prodigal Son					Families Forgiveness Good News	Homes
6. The Lost Sheep			Bridges	Building	Forgiveness	K. of H.
7. The Two Sons			Choices Witness	Messengers,	K. of H.	Good News,
8. The Sower		Growing	Beginnings			Growth, K. of H.
9. The widow's mite				Gifts Self Giving	Treasures K. of H.	Poverty
10. The Samaritan woman			Signs & Symbols	Signs & Symbols	Signs & Symbols	Water, Baptism, Faith
11. The paralytic						Faith, Friendship
12. Jesus calms the storm				Energy	Energy	Faith, Power of the Holy Spirit

K. of H. = Kingdom of Heaven

Jesus, Our Life poster series
THE BENEDICTINE NUNS OF TURVEY ABBEY

Part 1 **Jesus, Our Light**
This set of 11 posters tells the vivid story of Jesus' early life. These posters are ideal for use during Advent and Christmas.
11 Full colour laminated posters / Size: A2 / Ref: LOC1P
Includes double panel Nativity poster (A1)

Part 2 **Jesus, Our Way**
This set of 12 posters shows us the way Jesus leads us – through suffering and death to the glory of the Resurrection and the coming of the Holy Spirit. Twelve posters suitable for use at Lent & Easter.
12 Full colour laminated posters / Size: A2 / Ref: LOC2P

God's Promise
A set of 12 posters illustrating the power of the Old Testament. Starting at Genesis with a vibrant depiction of God's Creation and on to God's Blessing to Abraham and his people. Exodus follows with Moses receiving the Ten Commandments and then to Joshua and the story of the Promised Land. This colourful poster set carries on to illustrate some more of the fascinating stories from Scripture.
12 Full colour laminated posters / Size: A2 / Ref: POT1

1 Breath of the Spirit
2 Spirit Alive
SISTER SHEILA GOSNEY

Two striking sets of 8 full colour posters. The first is an ideal resource for confirmation programmes, the second expresses the external imagery of the Holy Spirit – Fire, Wind and Water the Dove – and other symbols of the life of the Christian church. Each poster, with the help of an accompanying booklet, may be used to explore the messages of the Scriptures.

Breath of the Spirit
8 Full colour laminated posters and guide booklet / Size: A2 / Ref: MPCP1
Spirit Alive
8 Full colour laminated posters and guide booklet / Size: A2 / Ref: MPSA

The Footsteps of Christ
THE BENEDICTINE NUNS OF TURVEY ABBEY

This popular set has been created from 16 glorious oil paintings by the Benedictine Nuns of Turvey Abbey. Suitable for Lent & Easter, the posters follow Christ along the journey of the Cross from Peter's denial to the entombment and ending with the joy and hope of the resurrection.
16 Full colour laminated posters (includes FREE book) / Size: A2 / Ref: FOCP